D0249257

Greek Painting

Compass History of Art

Collection under direction of André Held and D. W. Bloemena

The complete series includes

Greek Painting

Pierre Devambez

Curator of Greek and Roman Antiquities
at the Musée du Louvre

THE VIKING PRESS
New York

© 1962 by J. M. Meulenhoff Amsterdam

English translation © 1962 by George Weidenfeld and Nicolson Ltd.

Photographs © 1962 by André Held

Translated by Jean Steward

A COMPASS BOOKS original edition

Published in 1962 by The Viking Press, Inc.

626 Madison Avenue, New York 22, N.Y.

/

Library of Congress catalog card number: 62 – 12142

Printed in Holland

Contents

Greek painting

Introduction

The study of sculpture in Classical antiquity is one that can be undertaken without a sense of undue temerity; despite innumerable *lacunae*, the elements at the archaeologist's disposal are coherent enough to give some idea of the development of that art from Minoan to Roman times, particularly since its principles and its aims remained relatively constant.

Far more complex problems face the student who seeks to trace the development of painting during that period. One of the most serious difficulties lies in the lack of unity in a *genre* whose technique and aims underwent frequent alteration.

We may take the first phase as corresponding, broadly, to the civilization that grew up around the Aegean sea during the second millenium BC. Never, perhaps, in the whole of ancient times was painting so generally and whole-heartedly appreciated. Then, owing to historical circumstances, it disappeared completely for three or four centuries; familiar as we are today with abstract and non-figurative art, we can scarcely consider as painting the primitive network of geometric lines then used to decorate pottery. When painting revived again, it was merely in the form of drawing with added colour, very different from what the Minoans had produced and from what we ourselves understand by painting. It retained this form until the fourth century, by which time sculpture had already reached its apogee and even, according to one school of thought, was entering a period of decadence: a new school of painting then sprang up, which with its effects of light and shade and its variety of colouring was more closely akin to that of our own era. But we have no direct acquaintance with this fourth and third century painting, and know it only through the copies or adaptations made in Rome, and elsewhere in Italy, from the end of the first century BC.

Moreover such documentary evidence as we possess is scanty, and heterogeneous in character. There is no doubt that painting, even if it was not always equally appreciated, played an important part in artistic life throughout the whole of antiquity, save for that obscure period between the end of Mycenean and the beginning of Greek civilization. Both murals and separate pictures abounded, and we have textual evidence not only of the lasting fame of certain artists but of the public interest in everything to do with painting. Unfortunately these works have not survived: the pictures on wooden panels or canvasses naturally succumbed to the ravages of time, while the large-scale murals disappeared with the walls on which they were painted, or else, as was most frequently the case, when the mural was painted on a thin layer of stucco this crumbled away while the wall was still standing. A fortunate accident has enabled us to recover a number of sizable fragments of these mural paintings amid the ruins of Cretan palaces of the second millennium; but these are merely debris, which make us regret all the more keenly the paucity of our store, and yet which are of interest through the glimpses they provide of the trends of the time. It is to an accident, too, that we owe our possession of most of the Roman paintings we know: the masses of ash and lava under which they were buried in 63 AD kept intact, and even preserved, the wall paintings of Herculaneum and Pompeii. Nothing of the same sort kept intact the Greek works of the eighth to the second centuries BC.

However, in our attempt to reconstitute the pictorial art of this long period, we are fortunately not solely dependent on the vague and sketchy texts of ancient writers, which consist of imprecise descriptions and trivial anecdotes about painters and their works.

Every museum is well supplied with those painted vases which used to be known as Etruscan and which all, or practically all, are Greek or show Greek influence. The painting on these vases does not merely consist, as is the case elsewhere, of formal patterns serving a purely decorative purpose; almost from the beginning Greek vase-painting is narrative, descriptive or dramatic, and it is generally agreed that it often reproduces larger pictorial compositions, painted on walls or panels and displayed in sanctuaries or other public places. The transposition naturally alters the character of the original profoundly, but since until the fourth century large-scale painting appears to have used only a very few colours and to have been primarily dependent on drawing, the vase-paintings presumably offer a more faithful likeness (or at any rate less of a caricature) than if, say, David's *Consecration* were reproduced on a tea-set. We must also point out that the workmen whom potters entrusted with the decoration of their products were, on the whole, remarkable craftsmen and that some of them may even be described as incomparable artists.

Considering the paucity of our documentary evidence, we are entitled to eke out our knowledge of a school of painting in which draughtsmanship played a leading part, by reference to works executed in other media. Engravings on metal or (more rarely) on bone or ivory were popular in antiquity; these reveal some of the earliest and most interesting attempts to render perspective. From another point of view, there is a close connection between painting and bas-relief; the same subjects were frequently treated by both, and their problems of composition and layout are analogous. Moreover, on certain reliefs the outline of the figures has first been traced with a chisel—in other words, drawn in.

When we add to our list, moreover, the fairly plentiful store of tomb-paintings found in Etruria which, in technique if not in spirit, appear closely inspired by Greek art, it seems almost as if we had a superabundance of documentary evidence. In fact the difficulty arises from the heterogeneous character of this evidence, which in addition is indirect. The only original works we know are the remains of the Cretan frescoes. As regards strictly Greek art, we have nothing but reflected glimpses of actual painting; the pictures on the vases, which are often of great beauty, reveal the personality of the decorator who made them, and not that of the artist whose painting inspired them. And because they are copies, neither the Etruscan tomb-paintings nor the frescoes of Pompeii can be said to give us an exact idea of what Greek painting was really like.

Is this reason for giving up the attempt at the start? It is right to stress the risks and uncertainties of the undertaking; it is none the less tempting to surmount the obstacles and try to form some conception of that art which the men of antiquity valued so highly and which probably expressed, even better than literature or sculpture, certain important aspects of the life of the mind in ancient times. In the realm of Greek art, we know only reflections of that life.

Painting in Crete and Mycenae

During the course of nearly a millennium—from the end of the third century till almost the end of the second—there developed around Crete that brilliant civilization which we usually describe as Aegean or Pre-Hellenic. Sheltered from invasion, and yet close enough to the coastlines of Europe, Asia and Egypt, Crete was untroubled by wars, and being in a position, thanks to the navy which she had built up for herself, to maintain contact with the outer world, or to break it off at will, she acquired that wealth which forms such a suitable subsoil for the growth of the fine arts. Even when, by the beginning of the fourteenth century BC, Crete was no more than a province in that cultural nexus which centred on Mycenae, the civilization which she had created maintained its own individual personality, following the same ideals and subject to the same laws.

Painting was exceptionally favoured in Crete, and whilst there are few traces of sculpture surviving in the island—indeed there seems to have been no enthusiasm for it—the decoration of buildings no less than its more modest equivalent on pottery shows a feeling for line and colour unrivalled anywhere else at this time.

In the early phases of Cretan civilization we have to rely entirely on ceramics for our knowledge of this predilection. Possibly because they were trying to imitate the natural patina of stone—for like the Egyptians they used this material for their vases—the Cretans succeeded, by the use of a technique the secret of which is now lost, in adorning their earthenware with a whole gamut of delicate and changing tones ranging from the most delicate yellow to the deepest red. This is one of the outstanding features in the work of the Vassiliki school—so called from the excavations at that site which yielded a particularly rich harvest of specimens of this kind of work. It is a purely geometric art, similar to that which we find in the murals of the second millennium where the walls of houses are distempered in bright colours divided into irregular horizontal bands. At the same time however a feeling for decorative effects becomes apparent. Vases of this period begin to display—sometimes in light relief, sometimes in dark—motifs which though highly stylized are obviously derived from plant life and show a marked sureness of touch.

In the style associated with the site at Camares—a style which reached its apogee in the nineteenth century BC—vases are decorated in a manner which is cunningly and skilfully related to their form, with a rich polychrome in which red, orange, yellow and white predominate. It is a style which remains true to the tradition of the immediate past, relying on naturalistic themes with tiny squids and *nautili* as well as plant motifs.

From the beginning of the eighteenth century BC, however, this art—or should we call it a craft?—gives place to mural painting. The first palaces—and still more those which, in the seventeenth century, were rebuilt after some catastrophe, the precise nature of which is unknown to us—display, in their unfortunately mutilated remains, an astonishing richness and variety of decorative detail. There has been an especially rich yield at Knossos, which had become the capital city, the seat of Minos. These murals were painted on to the wet stucco, either directly on to the flat surface or, in imitation of a technique popular in Egypt at the time, by modelling figures in light relief and then colouring them. From Egypt too was derived the practice of painting the female figure white in contrast to the bronze-like colouring of the male. It would seem therefore that the artists of Crete learnt their *métier* from contacts with Egypt—a fact which is not really remarkable when one comes to think of the frequent relations established between the two countries.

But the Cretan debt to Egypt was confined to technique. The spirit and subject matter of this art were entirely different, and the Cretans maintained a marked independence in relation to their prototypes. Both the themes and their composition show a marked variety, with the human figure playing a dominant role, although not entirely displacing the representation of animal and vegetable life.

It is often difficult to determine which of these themes have a specifically religious character. The famous figure of the *Prince with the Lilies*, who seems originally to have been holding a griffon on the end of a leash, was probably a god. The long line of figures bearing offerings who stride in hieratic grandeur along one of the corridors of the palace of Knossos were no doubt engaged in some liturgical act. But what can we make of the dancers leaping into space? Are they merely performers displaying themselves for the delectation of the audience, or are they participating in some religious ceremony? And are the acrobats performing their hazardous contortions on the backs of bulls really engaged in some form of ritual tauromachy? If we confine ourselves to the purely pictorial aspect of these works, the answer to these questions is not one of vital importance, and in any case these figures who seem endowed with a specifically religious dignity are surrounded by a mass of others who are clearly assistants.

This visual suggestion of the presence of spectators is in fact one of the most curious characteristics of Cretan painting. A whole crowd of people throng the steps of the amphitheatre to watch the dances or bull fights; they are so numerous that sometimes the mass of spectators is not defined in detail but merely suggested by a few light silhouettes devoid of any sharp definition, against a dark background. Often however the figures are more sharply characterised and one can distinguish their individuality. This is especially so in the case of the celebrated *Parisienne*. This comparatively small figure, part of a larger composition, owes its name to the resemblance—noted immediately on its discovery in the early years of this century—to the *midinettes* so popular with

Toulouse-Lautrec. What strikes us about her is not only the details that make up her piquant beauty—the perky nose, the large eyes and sensual lips, the lock of hair hanging down over her forehead —but the bold technique of simplification which the artist has adopted; he has stressed only the essential features, those that give the most vivid, not the most photographic, likeness of the model; details that are not noticed at a first glance are deliberately sacrificed, and the ear, for instance, is not even suggested. This art anticipates Impressionism. And the *Parisienne*, if she may be considered the masterpiece of the genre, is by no means unique. In this respect Cretan art differs from all the other art of remote antiquity. And perhaps the Cretan preference for painting over sculpture was due to the greater vividness with which the former could render the fugitive character of figures and movements: Impressionist art, in our own time, worked with paintbrush and pencil.

In any case it would be difficult to imagine a livelier kind of art— vital in its depiction of gesture and pose, feeling and expression. In her apparent immobility the *Parisienne* seems to vibrate with impatience and curiosity, and when there is a scene which shows a group of people in a crowd, turning to each other and waving their arms, one almost seems to hear the noise of their chatter.

But this intensity of expression is not confined to human beings. We have already seen how nature—both animal and vegetable— was one of the main sources of inspiration for Cretan painting; even in the otherwise rather stiffly conceived frieze which adorns a building near the palace of Knossos, the pheasants and other crested birds are endowed with life and individuality. Even more remarkable, however, is the painting of a cat recently discovered at Hagia Triada. Hiding behind a bush, with its claws scrubbing the soil, its eyes dilated, its back arched, the animal is stalking a pheasant which struts innocently about, all unaware. Nothing could be more lifelike than this little scene. Even the bush is drawn with sensitive subtlety—as it sways in the wind it recalls the decorative purity of a Japanese drawing. The great charm of Cretan art lies in that suppleness and sense of movement which is shared by animate and inanimate creatures alike.

These paintings appear in many different varieties. There are frescoes so small that they might be described as miniatures— miniatures in relation to their size, of course, and not to their technique, for they have none of the delicacy of treatment which distinguishes this style; indeed it is these very frescoes which often contain the largest crowd scenes. But there are also paintings in which a whole wall or panel is taken up with figures of lifelike proportions. The procession of bearers to which we have referred consisted of figures on a large scale and the few poor remaining fragments from which we have had to reconstruct the figure of the *Prince with the Lilies* show that he must have been at least six feet high.

The *Prince with the Lilies* has been painted in a technique which shows clear Egyptian influence. It was not done directly on the wall but on a very light relief raised on the stucco with which the wall was covered—yet another link in the chain of contact between Crete and the valley of the Nile. This particular technique, however, is exceptional for the Island of Minos, and it is difficult to see what particular advantages it possessed. As it needed more work, it must have been more expensive, and it did not make the contours clearer. The individuality of Cretan painting lies in its colour— bright, bold and utterly independent of realism—making no bones even about painting a monkey blue. This disregard of realism surprises us mainly because we have difficulty in understanding the Cretan point of view. Just as they liked vivacity of movement, so they demanded that colour should be emotive, that it should be capable of brightening up a whole painting and making it more attractive. We must remember too that these pictures were intended to adorn apartments into which the light did not directly penetrate and in which strong colours were necessary to counteract the gloom.

The outstanding qualities which characterized mural painting are also to be found in ceramics, even though the relationship between these two art forms was not so close in Crete as it was to be in Greece. Cretan artists never adorned their vases with a formal composition, with human figures and a particular subject. They deliberately limited themselves to a form of decoration which, following the natural shape of the vase, pleased the eye without evoking real or imaginary scenes. Cretan vases lack the solidity and the strictly controlled proportions of Greek vases; the potters paid no attention to geometrical rules—they would hardly submit to the functional demands even of the object which they were creating. They were guided by their imagination alone. On the other hand the decorations on their vases were composed in such a way as to lay particular emphasis on the form which they adorned: a flowing form, incompatible with any sharply angular or abstractly geometrical design. On the convex surface of a full-bodied vase a squid will stretch out its long tentacles, seeming to embrace the vessel; on the long stem of a narrow *amphora*, the slender stalk of a plant forms an axis whence spring waving boughs; or tiny *nautili* are sprinkled on the brownish surface of the clay. But whatever scheme of decoration may be adopted, it never loses contact with real life or becomes a purely intellectual abstraction, even when—and this happened in the Palace style in the sixteenth century BC—a hardening and stylization take place and the fronded plants become mere spirals: the flowers and fish-life still form the basis of the decoration of the vases. Sometimes, as in the case of the *Prince with the Lilies*, this decoration is executed in relief, an indication that, despite differing sources of inspiration, relations between vase-painting and mural painting were close enough. But we are not faced with the problem which has to be solved in Greek archaic and classical art of whether the painters of the two were identical. Both are imbued with the same love of nature, but the mural artists depict it for itself alone, trying to convey to the onlooker something of the impressions which they would experience in contact with a living scene, in its natural setting. The vase-painters on the other hand use nature merely as an element, the sole purpose of which is to beautify the vase made by the potter for whom they work. Mural painting shows feeling: vase painting is above all else decorative.

Crete's isolation from the mainland did not last long. No doubt as soon as the tribes which had penetrated as far as the Peloponnese became stabilized, first of all commercial and then cultural contacts were established between them and the Cretans. If, nowadays, we refuse to believe that Mycenean civilization, which was centred on Argos, was nothing but a pale reflection of Cretan civilization, if we are prepared to credit it with its own personality and even a genuine originality, the fact still remains that without the help of Minoan civilization it could not possibly have developed as it did. Quite apart from anything else it showed no special interest in painting and, at least as far as we know, the Myceneans did not use murals in their palaces on the same generous scale that the Cretans did. It is in painting, too, that the identity of inspiration is most obvious. The same themes occur at Mycenae, Tiryns and Knossos: bull-fights and assemblies of women occur frequently, but there are also hunting scenes and processions of chariots—subjects to which Cretan artists paid no attention.

These paintings are not marked by the same freedom of treatment which characterises Cretan art, and though one can still recognize the skill with which they catch rapid movement and the fugitive pose, it is obvious that the artist's technical skill does not always match up to his ambitions. The most evanescent poses seem rigidly fixed. The picture of a boar flying in headlong panic, his four paws stretched out in an almost horizontal line, should convey a sense of insensate speed, whereas in fact the beast seems frozen by some magic force into an incomprehensible immobility. Perhaps because mural painting did not suit their temperament, artists seem to have taken more kindly to decorating earthenware vases. It was in Mycenae that two new shapes evolved, the round stirrup cup with a false mouth at the top, the real opening being at the side, and the 'champagne cup' with its slender foot supporting a graceful bowl. The decoration is now almost entirely restricted to sea-life, with the squid to which we have referred earlier playing a role of great importance. On other vases however —especially on rather clumsy-looking *kraters*—there appears for the first time a decorative scheme involving human figures—lines of chariots, warriors on the march, leaping bulls. There is no narrative, strictly speaking, involved, but there is a complete break with the traditional scheme of pure ornament for the decoration of ceramic ware. The two hitherto distinct fields of mural and craft painting are in the process of being merged, and just as the vase painters introduced into their work figures which formerly were only seen in frescoes, so one discovers on the walls of palaces nonrepresentational motifs of a kind which had previously been confined to the adornment of vessels or objects made from bronze.

This is a most important development, and one which may be thought to anticipate the narrative and dramatic figure-painting of purely Greek vases. In point of fact, of course, it would be extremely rash to draw any such conclusion. The paintings with which we are concerned belong to the fourteenth and thirteenth centuries, and human figures do not appear on Greek vases until the beginning of the eighth century at the very earliest. A gap of several centuries therefore must exist between these two art forms, and in the meantime a new civilization had been installed in the Greek world. Not only that, but Greek vase-painting—even in its most archaic form—starts off from quite a different spiritual approach, and aims at effects which are quite different from those which preoccupied the artists of Mycenae. What therefore, we might ask, had been happening in the interval, from the twelfth to the end of the ninth century—a period about which we know so little that it is sometimes called 'the dark ages of Greek art'?

The origins of Greek painting

In the course of the twelfth century and for several generations afterwards there became established in Greece a series of tribes which had migrated from Central Europe and the Danube basin. They probably differed little either by race or by language from their predecessors, who by the beginning of the second millennium had become established in the peninsula and had created Mycenean civilization. These invasions, however, not only created an atmosphere of insecurity and poverty, inimical to artistic growth, but they utterly destroyed the decadent culture which they already found in existence. These newcomers brought with them fashions which had already been apparent in Mycenae and which were diametrically opposed to those which had prevailed in Crete—a greater passion for exactitude, a less acute sense of the vitality of nature, a natural inclination towards order and a sense of geometrical form. No sooner had the first invaders appeared than the human form began to disappear from ceramic art, and at the same time the destruction of the royal palaces brought about that of mural art.

There is no need to describe the processes which transformed the formerly crude appearance of the vase into a solid and rational shape. We may, however, point out that the function of the decorative elements was to emphasize the structure of the vessel and bring out its proportions. Until the end of the ninth century this decorative scheme was to remain purely abstract, owing nothing to nature and deriving none of its stylized elements from any animal or vegetable motif. It was a purely geometrical art, and the skill of the artist lay almost exclusively in his power of arranging the composition—for long very loosely—and in the way in which he varied the not very numerous, but endlessly repeated elements which he had at his disposal—first of all circles, then angular lines forming triangles, lozenges and above all wavy lines and swastikas. These motifs appeared in black, a black which at first was dull and rather muddy, but later, as firing techniques improved, became sparkling against a background of terra cotta.

It is impossible to conceive of a more resolutely abstract art form; it was a kind of intellectual geometry, informed by a deep revulsion to all organic form. It was not until the beginning of the eighth century BC that religious beliefs conspired with special historical circumstances to introduce a new type of iconography. It was from Athens that there came an innovation which was destined to be decisive—the introduction of the human figure into abstract art. After an interval of centuries in which meaningless patterns had multiplied with varying success, Athenian artists started to reproduce the human figure. It was however a vastly different representation from that which had prevailed in Crete and Mycenae. To begin with, it was for long a simple hieroglyph made up of superimposed geometrical shapes—a sphere for the head, a triangle for the body, with the base forming the shoulders and the apex suggesting a fantastically slender waist, a trapezium for the arms, which in many cases were held up to the head as a sign of mourning. It would seem in fact that these early representations of the human figure were closely connected with funeral ceremonies. They are to be found on those large vases, placed on tombstones, which served both as commemorative monuments for people of distinction and receptacles for containing the libations which, according to the funeral rites then prevailing, were poured down the throats of those who had died. It was natural enough that there should be a preference for depicting on these vases a representation of the funeral rites rather than mere decorative ornament: it was at least reassuring for everybody—including the corpse—to know that they had been properly observed. The most conspicuous place in the composition was therefore occupied by the corpse, stretched out on a bier, while around stood the obligatory crowd of hired mourners engaged in their customary task. The whole picture was intended to serve as a kind of epitaph, and the memory of the inhabitant of the tomb was perpetuated by battle-scenes similar to those in which he had participated when still alive. These scenes, however, did not entirely displace the geometrical elements, and the artist distributed a wealth of zig-zags, wavy lines and swastikas not only around the outside of the composition but even within the picture space. At about the same time there appeared another motif, also purely ornamental and derived no doubt from the East, composed of animals, either in isolation or in a frieze—usually deer or sea-birds.

From the moment that the human figure began to appear, for ritualistic and funerary purposes, it became inevitable that it would be used for other purposes. The eighth century was the age of the epic and of the mythical story. On vases which could not have been intended for the religious uses which these other large earthenware receptacles had served, we find stories about heroes, scenes of rape and combat, or those stately processions which took place at ceremonies in honour of the gods and of departed heroes. At first human beings are represented, as they were on the large funerary vases, in a very stylized fashion—but as the artist comes to depict precise occasions he tends to give his figures a more individualized appearance. Generalities disappear before the particular.

Athens was undoubtedly the initiator of this new development, which was to bring forth such abundant riches. It was from the most important of the Athenian necropolis, Dipylon, that there were unearthed those colossal vases on which the human figure appears for the first time, and from deposits in the smaller tombs we can follow the early development of this style. Soon these innovations were spreading all over the Greek world, and soon living figures, both animal and human as well as flowers, began everywhere to supplant abstract ornament.

Despite its renown Attic art did not play a determining role in this stylistic development. Foreign influences were more marked, especially from the East, from Syria and Egypt, for Greece had come into close contact with these countries as a result of the colonizing movement which began in the eighth century. It was from these sources that Greek artists derived the motifs which they were to use to ornament their vases. From their long journeys to the Far East sailors brought back carpets, embroidered silks, textiles and inlaid coffers, decorated with stylized plants, birds, animals of every kind, lions, panthers and mythological monsters such as the griffin and the sphinx. The strangeness of these ornaments, their rich colours and their technical sophistication made a natural and inevitable appeal to a people who were beginning to be bored with the austere Puritanism of the geometric style. It was naturally the great ports and harbours which served as the starting points from which these influences were to spread and around which they were to achieve their most intense expression. But they were by no means limited to these areas, and soon spread to regions far removed from the great sea-routes. Following Corinth and Rhodes, Athens and Sparta began to copy the fashion—to such an extent that the whole of the eighth century is often known as the 'Orientalising Period'.

This Oriental influence however did not follow a uniform pattern everywhere and it is not difficult to differentiate beween separate studios, each having its well-defined style.

Rhodes mainly produced dishes and large pot-bellied jugs for serving wine, provided for this purpose with a mouthpiece with three lips for ease in pouring the contents into a bowl or cup. It is probable that this shape was copied from that of the more expensive metal vases of which only a very few examples survive, but in both cases the decoration is obviously derived from oriental textiles with their narrow, parallel bands of ornament. Arranged in a continuous line, or sometimes facing each other in a heraldic fashion, are animals which the artist treats as individual entities, uncontaminated by any communal relationship. An ibex can lie cheek by jowl with a lion in absolute safety—for what counts is the decorative effect, the purity of line, the splashes of colour. Actually one cannot use the word polychrome in this context. The surface of the vase is covered with a fine ivory-tinted slip which throws into relief the blackness of the varnish used to outline the figures. Certain details—heads especially—are more or less left alone, being hinted at rather than expressed, with a very light brush stroke. Touches of white and deep red are scattered about to throw into relief such details as hair or wings. But the technique is often as detailed as that of a miniaturist, in which nothing is left to chance and in which spots of colour appear at the precise places where they contribute most to the general tonal harmony. Often however the design is on a more generous scale and two figures appearing in juxtaposition on a vase emphasize its formal pattern and are endowed with a certain monumentality.

At Corinth, which by virtue of its geographical position was in contact both with the Aegean and the Far East, with the Adriatic and with the Greek colonies in Italy and Sicily, potters worked mainly for the export market, and it was only later that they began to produce the larger type of vase. Throughout the seventh century they specialized in small-scale vases and especially in those phials in which the manufacturers of their country retailed the perfumed oils of which Corinth was then the main producer. The shape of these vases is not original: those known as *alabastron*, which are elongated in shape, derive from Egyptian prototypes, while the pattern known as *aryballos*, which is roundbellied, is of a type which we have already found in Crete. Both were used by athletes to pour oil on their bodies before and after indulging in violent exercise, which is the reason why they have narrow mouths and a flat surrounding lip which served to spread on the oil.

These small-scale vessels did not offer much scope for decoration. The first kind to appear consisted of an isolated figure—a bird or fish. Then quite suddenly towards the middle of the seventh century a style developed which made use of the human figure, and did so with such success that it is sometimes known as 'the magnificent style'. Vases, whose total height seldom exceeded two or three inches, were adorned with parallel bands of figures, some depicting a hunting scene, others a plaited pattern or a design of running dogs, another a battle. The scenes containing human figures, designed on a minute scale, are capable of endless enlargement, for not only is the draughtsmanship perfect but the whole conception is often on a monumental scale, while at the same time there is a decorative sureness of touch about the figures, usually depicted in silhouette. If we examine the Chigi *oinochoe* (the *oinochoe* is a jug, often with a handle rising above the level of the neck, used for pouring out the drinks which had been mixed in the larger *krater*), which, although it is on a larger scale, is divided into a number of decorative zones, we see a troop of warriors advancing to the sound of a trumpet with the delicate precision of a *corps de ballet:* the linear precision is absolute, and no less happy is the general mass-effect, so that equal pleasure may be derived either from inspecting an isolated figure or from viewing the whole group of figures as a decorative unit.

This style, known as the Protocorinthian, survived for only a short time. Probably it demanded too great an expenditure of time and trouble, especially as there was a great demand for ware of this kind—a demand which had to be satisfied as quickly and as cheaply as possible. There was a return, therefore, to motifs derived from Asiatic sources—lions and panthers and occasionally the Oriental goddess of the animal world or some anthropomorphic creature.

It is possible that Crete played a key role in the transmission of Asiatic influences. Cretan artists were in any case prolific in their experiments and in their discovery of technical processes which in the long run were to benefit all Greece. It would seem that they were the first to transpose into ceramics the metalworkers' technique of incision, scratching with a needle the surface of the black-varnish glaze to bring out within the contours of the rather vague silhouetted figures streaks of the earth-coloured background, to show up details such as the face, the muscular structure or clothing.

It was they too who, though only for a short time, started a fashion for polychrome, making use not only of red, black and white, but of more delicate shades such as yellow and blue. Nor is there any need to digress about the complicated and exotic shapes into which they fashioned the vessels they were to adorn. It comes as something of a surprise to discover that this Cretan school, for all its lively inventiveness, had so short a span of existence.

Equally short, too, were the lives of the different schools which grew up on different parts of the Cyclades. During the whole of the seventh century workshops of great distinction on these islands produced themes and evolved forms which, though impregnated with Asiatic influences, still showed great originality and threw into relief their superb craftsmanship. An attempt has been made —not always with any degree of certainty—to distinguish between the schools of Paros and Naxos, which seem to have been the two most important, especially if Paros was in fact the homeland of that style which in the past has been thought of as Milesian. It was a style at once delicate and monumental, informed by a decorative instinct which expressed itself with equal ease in the isolated figure of a real or fantastic animal, as in large mythological compositions, and by a knowing certainty in the disposition of colour—qualities characteristic of a school which would have seemed destined for a more glorious future than it did actually have.

For a long time it was the general opinion that the seventh century was a period of decadence for both pottery and painting. This is not so but, as the Athenian potters seem to have worked only for a local market and did not, like the Corinthians or the Rhodians, export their products to Italy, it has been necessary to wait until excavations in Greece itself were organized on a sufficiently scientific basis to reap an unexpected harvest of riches.

This art, known as Protoattic, preserved in the seventh century the traditions of the geometric style. The harsh stylized vigour of the Dipylon figures was not however maintained; on the contrary we see the Protoattic potters, painfully and clumsily it is true, but tenaciously and eventually successfully, seeking to endow the figures which they represent with a plasticity, an individuality and a consistency which gradually removes them from abstraction and brings them close to life. There can be no doubt that the epics with their sharply characterized heroes—think of Ulysses—had a decisive effect on pictorial art in this respect. When he depicted a scene the artist wanted his audience to be able to recognize it, and as he knew himself to be incapable of achieving this result by artistic means alone he would write the names of the main characters beside them.

But the traditions of the eighth century BC survive mainly in the monumental character of the scenes depicted, and in their composition. The Athenians who, as we have already pointed out, did not at this period export their ceramics, were in a position to manufacture vases which though less colossal than those of the past were still large enough, and of impressive proportions. And instead of using the space at their disposal to multiply different incidents or produce bands of decoration, they filled all the available space with a single image—gripping the attention of the spectator and dominating his interest. Although this image might be purely decorative, the tendency was for it to become narrative or dramatic. Oriental influences are apparent and show themselves in a new interest in flowers and above all in real or fantastic animals. One feels however that this influence is alien to the spirit of the artists and that its effect is superficial.

Consciously or unconsciously, they tend to revert to subjects in which man—or gods made in his image—dominate the decorative area.

These tendencies were not confined to ceramics. As one looks at some of the scenes on these vases one realises that behind them must have been a tradition of pure figure-painting, and this notion receives support from evidence which, though meagre, is most significant. In one of the more remote regions of Greece, at Thermum in Aetolia, the ruins of several temples—the oldest of which probably goes back to the ninth century—have been discovered, and in one of them is a series of fictile metopes (the spaces between the holes in which the beams of the roof were embedded —the *opae*—were known as *metopes*, i.e. between *opae*, and were one of the most obvious sites for decorative display. The word was also used to describe the face of a crab) which were not sculpted, as was usually the case, but painted. The technique is exactly the same as that used on vases, the figures being painted on a clay panel which was then fired—but the colours are more numerous and more varied. The metopes do not present any overall unity of design—each one deals with a different subject, the most famous and the best preserved being that which shows Perseus in flight after killing Medusa—a subject which from this point onwards was destined to have a great iconographical popularity in Greece. The metopes themselves are attributed to the middle of the seventh century. Other subjects occupy the rest of the series—people talking to each other—a hunter returning with his prey, and Aedon about to be turned into a nightingale by Zeus. The survival of these metopes proves that monumental painting did exist during the Orientalising period, that it counted amongst its practitioners artists of importance, and that henceforward we are justified in seeking in the decoration of vases a reflection of an art which at one time must have been seen not only on friezes, divided up into metopes, but also on pediments and on the entire surfaces of walls which have been destroyed by the passage of time.

Archaic painting

In the fields of both painting and ceramics as well as in the other arts, the seventh century had been a period of experimentation. The following century however was one of stabilization. Round about 600 BC there had been numerous schools, each with its own mark of originality which distinguished it from the rest. A hundred years later there was only one school of importance—Athens. At the end of the seventh century a process was evolved—the black figure technique—which was adopted by nearly every practising artist. The figures were entirely covered with a coat of varnish, and would have been almost impossible to distinguish if the artists had not picked out such details as clothes, hair and women's skins with splashes of white or dark red, and had not by fine, incised lines emphasized the outline of the muscles and the fall of drapery. Towards 530 BC, however, another technique begins to emerge in which the figures, in the reddish colour of the clay, stand out against a dark background while details picked out by brushwork give them a perfect visual clarity. Throughout the seventh century the main tendency was towards order and logic.

It was a century too which saw simultaneously great strides in the development of mural painting. Nothing survives of this, but a literary tradition ascribes the origins of the movement to this century and it is during this period that the decoration of vases shows, more vividly than in the past, the influence of prototypes which can only have been frescoes or monumental paintings.

The disappearance of these schools which were ultimately vanquished by Athens only took place in stages, and with the exception of the Cretan all these schools which we have mentioned before were still flourishing. There were other schools too which in the course of the century were to have a considerable influence and which were to shine with some glory—though only for a short time. And we must emphasize the fact that their disappearance was probably due rather to external causes than to any germ of decay within themselves which might have condemned them to a premature end.

We shall only discuss briefly the schools which flourished in Asia Minor and in the islands of the Aegean. They carried on the traditions of the seventh century and we find on *oenocho* attributed to Rhodes bands of grazing animals. Generally the ceramic ware of these schools retains and even accentuates the rather rustic feeling which it had always shown, and we might wonder at the small part played by the human figure and narrative in the work of these Ionic islanders who had a real taste for narrative and anecdotal elements, were it not for the evidence of a limited but interesting group of works known as 'The *Hydriae* of Caere' (the modern Cerveti in Italy. A *hydria* was a three-handled pitcher for carrying water from the well) which seem to reveal new and more interesting aspects of this school.

The thirty or so vases which belong to this series all come from Caere, but it would seem that the painting—unique of its kind in our opinion—even if it became native to Etruria, derived originally from the coast of Asia Minor. The vases are all of the same rather heavy, rustic pattern, and they would be entirely devoid of interest were it not for the strange originality of their decoration. This consists almost entirely of epic or mythological scenes, which in itself is not surprising, but the artist has treated these with a passion for detail, often of a humorous or amusing character, which has no parallel in the work of any other school. He was endowed with an ability to seize on telling details, and with malicious naïvety he transposed into everyday life scenes which by their inherent grandeur should have been far removed from it. Hercules, one of his favourite characters, appears sometimes as a rather ridiculous swashbuckling type, sometimes as a rather stupid but well-meaning giant. Zeus and Apollo are treated with scant respect, and the grouping of the various figures in a scene—even when they are gods—seems based on the pattern of everyday life. The drawing is a little slack, but each figure seems endowed with an internal vitality which gives it expression and life. Finally, we can tell from some of the specimens which are not too badly damaged that the painter of these *hydriae* was a colourist of rare ability who used the few shades at his disposal to give his works an entirely unexpected vivacity and gaiety. We know from internal evidence that in the sixth century there flourished in Ionia a school which had a well-deserved reputation for its excellence, and it is more than possible that the *hydriae* of Caere evince something of its spirit, and that the qualities displayed by our humble artist were the same which, displayed in larger works, compelled the admiration of pilgrims at Ephesus and the other great shrines of Eastern Anatolia.

We could not however go so far as to draw similar conclusions from a study of the ceramic ware actually manufactured in the islands of the Aegean. Those which attract our attention are essentially the work of artists whose talents, and they were very real ones, consisted in being able to set in just the right place the appropriate figure, whose significance derived from the precision of its outline and the arrangement within that outline of the appropriate coats of paint and of suitably placed highlights. The drinking cups made at Chios demonstrate this style in its perfection—but they throw no light on the painting of the period.

Can we say the same about a most unusual cup, now in the Louvre, the background of which is taken up by what we could hardly call a landscape, but which is, at any rate, one of those rare pictures which Greek artists of the pre-Hellenic period seem to have painted with no other object than that of expressing their delight in the nature which surrounded them? The composition may seem a little odd. The painter wanted to depict a man in a forest: to show his happiness he has made him wave his arms and open his mouth as though he were singing as he runs about. But to adapt the composition to the circular frame of the medallion the artist has arranged his trees not vertically but horizontally, so that they are perpendicular to the human figure; the branches curve over, following the circumference. To complete the landscape there are nests at the top of the tree-trunks with birds fluttering towards their young ones. The difficulty of enclosing within a circle a picture of this sort (designed to be displayed breadthwise), the clumsiness of the artist who was only able to solve the problem by flattening out his trees, prove that this must be an adaptation, since the subject could not have been designed for its present form. It is thus tempting to conclude that a picture must have served as model for the decorator of the cup, and this picture may well have been Ionian, since in the world of Greece only the Ionians seem to have appreciated natural beauty.

Equally interesting, though from a different point of view, is the evidence about the larger paintings provided by the cups of the Laconian school. We did not think it necessary, when speaking of the seventh century, to mention the somewhat unsophisticated ceramics made in Sparta, but in the sixth century the Laconian school produced some rather interesting pottery, which was moreover popular enough to be exported abroad. Of this output we shall only consider the cups: the bowl, mounted on a long slender stem, is decorated on the outside with a purely formal pattern, but on the inner surface the medallion displays, with black figures on a ground coated with a whitish slip, some scene which most frequently seems to reproduce a painting. This is particularly noticeable on a cup in the Berlin Museum: warriors are striding forward in pairs, bearing on their shoulders the body of one of their companions; this group occupies the centre of the medallion, but on the sides, right and left, we see the beginning of two identical groups cut off by the frame less than halfway across; it is not difficult to imagine a vast mural panel on which bands of soldiers returning from battle were thus depicted marching in procession; here the decorator has extracted one fragment without considering the space at his disposal. Other scenes, more skilfully composed, must also have been inspired by larger paintings, such as Prometheus being torn by the eagle, and even more the very curious representation of Arkesilas, King of Cyrene, supervising the weighing of sylphium, a plant that grew in his country and provided a profitable source of revenue for the throne. Here the composition is particularly skilful: whereas in works of this sort, in order that the figures may be set out on a horizontal line, the medallion is usually divided by a line into two unequal sections, the upper part being reserved for the figured scene and the lower occupied by a subsidiary pattern. In this cup the horizontal line has been used to suggest the deck of the boat on which King Arkesilas watches the operation, while the lower part quite naturally corresponds to the hold where slaves are loading bags containing the precious product. It was doubtless Sparta's policy of deliberate austerity and self-segregation that, before the end of the seventh century, cut short the development of this flourishing ceramic industry.

On the other hand, the history and the character of vase-painting in Corinth and Athens are largely explained by the stages of their commercial rivalry. We saw that the two schools, during the course of the eighth century, displayed equal brilliance in very different styles. Whereas Athens confined herself to producing articles for her own population, Corinth worked chiefly for the foreign market; each of the two schools pursued its own line, and mutual influences were scanty. The situation changes in the early years of the sixth century; and we can discern, in the work of the potters as well as in that of the decorators, an obvious wish to confuse distinctions in the mind of the public and thus attract to themselves, more or less unconsciously, the clientèle of the rival school. Thus the Corinthians, without abandoning the production of small scent-vases decorated with traditional patterns, began to make huge *kraters* whose bodies were adorned with scenes representing chiefly banquets, battles, or grotesque Dionysiac dances. The type was one popular in Attica; the difference lies in the arrangement of the decoration. The Athenians set it out broadly, filling all the space at their disposal with a single subject; the Corinthians treat a variety of themes, each occupying a relatively narrow zone, enclosed above and below by other zones containing other subjects. On the other hand, the cups of which this school was to produce such perfect examples seem, in Attica, to have been originally imitated from a form current in Corinth. As for themes and motifs, we notice that these, too, were transmitted from one school to the other. Palmettes, lotus flowers, little chains make their appearance towards the beginning of the seventh century in Athens, where they were unknown, it seems, during the Orientalising period. Corinth did not ignore living figures, far from it, but her artists and their customers had a predilection for monsters, wild beasts and birds, rather than for the human figure; the 'magnificent' Protocorinthian style of which we have spoken constituted in this respect, as in several others, a somewhat puzzling sort of parenthesis. The Athenians, for their part, were probably bowing to fashion when they painted on their vases in the seventh century lions or wolves, sirens or sphinxes, but their tastes indubitably led them to represent human beings, to illustrate familiar scenes of myth and epic; it was only in the later style of the seventh century that, precisely in imitation of Corinth, the representation of animals acquired an importance which it did not long retain.

By about 575 BC the two schools seem to have reached a point where, each having taken from the other whatever might be of use to it, the conflict between them entered on its final phase, which was to end some twenty-five years later with the complete and final obliteration of the Corinthian studios so far as ceramics were concerned. It was about 575 that the Corinthians took to spreading on their vases, before firing them, a reddish slip that gave the clay the identical look of Attic earthenware; it was at the same period that they began deliberately to replace their traditional representations of dances and banquets by legendary scenes in the Attic manner: the murder of Tydeus, the lament of the Nereids over the body of Achilles, the departure to the wars of the seer Amphiaraos. At the same period, the Athenians, for the first time in our knowledge, despatched a vase of great price into Etruria, a *krater* divided into zones in the Corinthian style; this vase is known as the François vase, after its discoverer. The interest we take in it would not have surprised the men of antiquity; indeed the potter who shaped it and the painter who decorated it were sufficiently proud of their work to set their signatures on this *krater*, several times over: Kleitias and Ergotimos. It has been described as a sort of Bible of Greek antiquity; an amazing number and variety of subjects are depicted all round the foot and body and neck of the vase in narrow bands laid one above the other, and even the handles are decorated with figures; if some of the patterns show Corinthian influence, the taste for storytelling is typically Attic. Such an Athenian legend as Theseus landing at Delos is prominently displayed; the other themes belong to common stock. Chief among them are Calydon's hunt, the murder of Troilos by Achilles, above all the marriage of Thetis and Peleus; somewhat out of sight near the bottom of the vessel is a grotesque battle between cranes and pygmies, reminiscent of the Batracomyomachia wrongly attributed to Homer. The variety, the abundance, the lack of unity of the whole thing are somewhat disconcerting. But if one looks at the *krater* as a whole one's eye is not offended, for this diversity blends in a harmony of lines and colours; a closer inspection yields the delight of studying each of the pictures in detail, of reading the inscriptions lavishly provided by the painter to prevent any confusion in the spectator's mind, and in admiring the ingeniousness of the composition, the liveliness of the attitudes, the skill with which the draughtsman, aware of the deficiencies of his technique, has skirted the difficulties of his art.

Other works of somewhat different character bear the signature of the painter Kleitias, but the inspiration of the François *krater* can be recognized in other vase-paintings, many of which seem to reproduce murals: for instance that of Perseus hunted by the Gorgons, on a vase in the Louvre of somewhat monumental character. About 550 the output of Corinthian studios, which had hitherto seemed to rival those of Athens, stopped suddenly; true, the Ionian and Laconian schools already mentioned were still flourishing, as was another which we can only mention, the 'Chalcidian' school, probably centred round the Straits of Messina; but none of these were sufficiently important to cause any anxiety among Attic workers, who remained in sole control of the market. Two tendencies can henceforward be distinguished in Attic art, coexisting as equal rivals: on the one hand a taste for grandeur and nobility, already apparent in the Geometric period and in many works of the seventh century; on the other a certain tendency to mannerism, preciosity and refinement.

This second tendency is amply represented under the reign of the tyrant Peisistratos and his sons, who sought, by fostering luxury, to divert the aristocracy from political preoccupations and from their natural antagonism to a dictatorial regime that had deprived them of their prerogatives. The mass arrival of Ionians, driven by wars or by revolutions from the cities of Asia Minor, helped to spread throughout Attica a taste for luxurious living. It is scarcely surprising, then, that potters produced so large a number of these elegant, delicate vases with sharp-edged brims, each adorned with a single clear-cut figure, drawn with a miniaturist's precision, which by the very fact of standing alone against the ruddy earthenware assumes an almost monumental dignity. This is the Little Masters' art, which is displayed not only on *kylixes* but on all sorts of forms: thus the work of a potter named Amasis, probably of Egyptian origin—*amphorae*, cups, jars, and those slender phials known as *lekythes*—was decorated by an anonymous painter with scenes of every sort; we see that Oriental goddess who protected wild animals, but also scenes of licentious revelry, Dionysos surrounded by dancing Maenads and so forth; and whether gods or mortals are portrayed, whether the figures are calm or lively, the dominant characteristic is always an almost excessive refinement, a studied grace of attitude that sometimes verges on affectation.

The works of Exekias are inspired by a very different spirit. There is always an element of grandeur about them; some of the scenes he depicts seem borrowed from everyday life, but he succeeds, without detracting from their naturalness, in conferring nobility upon them, not only by giving illustrious names to the actors in these scenes—Castor and Pollux, or Ajax—but moreover by bringing out the profoundly human element in the most ordinary actions. Two young men leaving for the wars and saying farewell to their parents are called the Dioscuri; there is no theatrical lamentation, no anecdotic detail, but the whole thing is full of a quiet gravity that gives grandeur to an incident personally experienced by all Athenians. A man thrusts into the ground the sword on which he is about to fling himself in self-destruction; his attitude is that of any gardener planting seeds, but this gardener is called Ajax, and one is struck by the contrast between so ordinary an action and the tragic destiny of the man who deliberately performs it. Many of Exekias' works show battles, those of Herakles in particular. But one work deserves special consideration, a cup which at any rate by its lay-out bears some resemblance to that Ionian vessel showing a man in a wood: in the centre of a medallion that takes up the whole of the bottom of the cup, Dionysos is pictured in a small boat, with a full sail whose mast has miraculously turned into a grapevine. The sea is suggested symbolically by a shoal of fish or dolphins swimming swiftly all round the frame, enclosing within their dance the boat on which a god is sailing. Nothing could be simpler or less like a seascape, but this suggestive yet wholly unrealistic sketch creates a powerfully poetic impression. Exekias and the Amasis painter, however, are by no means the only Attic representatives of that art of vase-painting which enjoyed unprecedented fame not only locally but throughout the Mediterranean world; every site showing the influence of Greek culture yields its harvest of Little Master vases, and the great vessels exported to Etruria were popular in the cities of Asia Minor and Syria.

This prolific output none the less comprises many works of the highest quality, and in spite of the inconvenience of the shapes on which the artist had to work, we often have the impression of a painting made to be looked at flat on a wall. And yet black-figure, the only process then in use, was not that employed in larger paintings; these were done with varied colours against a light background. On the vases, on the contrary, the figures are always silhouettes, picked out here and there with a touch of crimson or white, and with no other means of defining anatomy or expression than lines incised on the hard surface of already fired clay. One can but marvel at the way in which, working with means so unfavourable for expressiveness or even for precision, the artists so frequently attained a degree of mastery that enabled them to interpret as they chose the most varied feelings: from the refined elegance of the Amasis painter to the touching grandeur of Exekias, there is not a single nuance that escapes them.

And yet their rendering always remained a little superficial: for how could they convey the deeper feelings, the hesitancies and varying states of mind of characters seen only as black silhouettes? An apparently quite simple invention, a technical improvement, was to open up new ways to vase-painters, enabling them to probe deeper into psychology. The black glaze with which hitherto the figures had been covered was now used merely to outline them, or else, laid on with the single hair of a very fine brush, to suggest the details formerly incised with a graver's needle: the lines thus acquired greater precision and the figure, now light instead of dark, became far easier to understand. This new process, known as red-figure, was introduced into potters' workshops about 535; it was to remain in use until about the end of the fourth century, when vases ceased to be decorated with figured scenes.

Fruitful as this invention proved, it did not represent any break in the development of vase-painting; for at least a generation, certain artists used either process impartially, the themes remained identical and the new technique was still too much in its infancy for those who practised it to know how to take advantage of all its potentialities. It is none the less true that, since it was easier to practise—the brush being more readily handled than the graver's needle—and because its effect on the eye was lighter and more cheerful, the number of vase-painters suddenly increased while that of their customers, already considerable, was further multiplied. Let us mention only two names among so many: Oltos, who specialised in cups, and Euphronios, who worked in a wider field and who, beginning as a mere draughtsman in the service of a merchant, was later able to afford his own studio, where he employed younger decorators. Both of these artists were fond of epic themes and belonged to that heroic tradition that had inspired many black-figure masterpieces. Other artists chose rather to represent scenes likely to please a clientèle of youthful aristocrats: banquets with all their accompanying amusements, scenes of athletic training or competition.

For about fifty years, until the time when the Persians, in 478, saw their ambitious plans collapse and left Greek soil, vase-painting reached its apogee in the history of Greek art. Here again it is difficult to gauge the influence of larger paintings. We know that many artists practising the latter were highly thought of in antiquity, but we know little else about them: Kimon of Kleonai, praised by Pliny, is a mere name to us today.

Better than any explanation, the illustrations in this book will give some idea of the art of certain painters of whom many are anonymous, but some of whom did sign their works. Among dominant figures in their time were the Kleophrades painter and the Berlin painter, the artist who worked for the potter Brygos, Douris and Makron; many traces of archaism can be found in their work: the subjects they treat, among which battles predominate; certain peculiarities in their draughtsmanship, which shows an occasional clumsiness, added to a sort of joyful zest for life which is the attribute of a youthful nation. And these themes are treated with unprecedented depth and dramatic sense: the fighting warriors no longer slash at one another mechanically, they have become human beings, with human thoughts; and the drawing, if it does not quite succeed in rendering all the subtleties of anatomy or drapery, is none the less done with a rare sureness of touch, a forcefulness, that were not to be found in black-figure work; and the composition now follows a rhythm which, without artificial symmetry, balances cunningly grouped masses in a way that wholly satisfies the mind. There is perhaps no other example in the whole of Greek art of details so perfect in themselves and yet so intelligently subordinated to the essential effect of the whole.

The introduction of red-figure had, if not completely abolished, at any rate greatly reduced the part played by heightening touches of red and white, so frequent in black-figure. Larger painting, however, must certainly have continued to use a variety of colours. In imitation of this, the artisans who decorated vases inaugurated a technique which had already been tried out, although not persevered with, by workshops other than those of Athens, at the beginning of the sixth century. A white coating was laid on the surface of the vase, and on this coat were drawn in outline figures which were then coloured red, brown, yellow, and probably green and blue. This technique could only be used for vessels that served no practical purpose, since any contact with liquid would have dissolved this fragile colouring. And so this process was only used in exceptional cases, for vases offered to the dead or consecrated to the gods in their sanctuaries. To this we owe, on the cups of this period and later on funerary *lekythoi*, a number of masterpieces combining the traditional purity of draughtsmanship with a shimmering brilliance of colour.

We owe to it, moreover, a clearer understanding than we could get from vases decorated in the usual way of the real character of larger painting; for this, too, made use of varied colours against a white ground, and was certainly envisaged primarily as drawing, enlivened by colour—red and brown and violet—and knew nothing of the effects of gradations of tone.

Now several of the painters most highly esteemed in antiquity were alive at this period, in the years before the middle of the fifth century. Most famous of all was Polygnotos, a native of Thasos, a small northern island, son of a painter who had enjoyed a certain reputation even outside his own province. Polygnotos practised his art in different parts of Greece, particularly in Delphi and at Athens, where the ruling class thought highly of him, and where he produced important decorations; nothing is left of his work save some descriptions, often detailed and yet quite inadequate to give us any idea of his talent. He had painted battles, but his two most famous compositions were the murals in the assembly room (the *Lesche*) of the Knidians at Delphi. These displayed on one side the sack of Troy by the Greeks and on the other Odysseus' visit to Hades; two episodes borrowed from epic literature, one from the now lost poem of the *Little Iliad*, the other from the *Odyssey*.

We should doubtless find these paintings disconcerting; not only on account of the mass of inscriptions identifying various characters, or of the flat arbitrary colouring, akin to that on the white-ground vases, but also because of the hitherto unfamiliar arrangement of the figures in registers one above the other—or rather in irregular tiers, which the painter has tried to make more convincing by suggesting unevennesses in the ground which would account for some figures having their feet on a level with others' shoulders. One can hardly use the term landscape, since only the contour is suggested by a fine line, and if Polygnotos has happened to place trees here and there, it is because their presence was essential to define and explain the scene. The arrangement is in fact theatrical, coinciding, not by chance, with the popularity of Aeschylean and Sophoclean tragedy. There is a relation between the way Polygnotos' figures are set out on various levels, and the actual grouping on the Greek stage: the chorus circling round the altar, in the orchestra, the actors declaiming on their platform, and the *Deus ex machina* perched on the roof of the stage. Another invention attributed to Polygnotos also smacks of the theatre: he was, it was said, the first to give varied expressions to his faces, showing lips twisted in pain, eyes raised heavenward in despair; and here again one is reminded of those exaggeratedly expressive masks that actors assumed when reciting their roles. The interest in facial expression corresponds moreover to the psychological studies which the great playwrights of the time were making fashionable. If Aristotle described Polygnotos as the most ethical of all painters, it was because he sought to depict human emotions on the faces he portrayed. We should only have a faint notion of these innovations were it not for the fact that in the master's lifetime, vase-painters were already seeking to imitate him and make use of his technique. A famous *krater* in the Louvre, which shows on one side the murder of the Niobides, on the other warriors preparing for an expedition, seems to be a faithful copy of the newest processes. A *kylix* in Munich attains great intensity in the rendering of emotion: the medallion shows Achilles killing Penthesileia, Queen of the Amazons, and at the very moment when his sword is piercing her, Achilles looks at his adversary and realises too late that they love one another.

The sudden introduction of these psychological factors was to change the relations hitherto existing between large-scale painting and vase-painting: the growing gulf between them was due not to technical difficulties but to the complication and refinement of themes; psychological subtleties were beyond the scope of decorators who, though skilful, were pressed for time, and perhaps the average clientèle of the potters preferred somewhat less complex subjects.

And yet the themes used in industrial art were changing too. The great painters of the early years of the century had imparted an atmosphere of nobility to a wide range of subjects: the most ordinary, even trivial scenes—athletic exercises, banquets with their unfortunate consequences, children at school—had acquired a dignity that was not incompatible with liveliness. Henceforward, perhaps because a different social class was coming to the fore in Attica while the aristocratic way of life began to decay, vase-paintings show familiar scenes treated with greater attention to the petty aspects of existence. Family life, domestic occupations, the practice of arts and crafts provided a new store of themes which were abundantly exploited. Very soon, corresponding to a social transformation that alarmed traditionalists, the clientèle frequenting potters' shops became largely feminine. Middle-class Athenian housewives were the customers for whom vases were now fashioned in novel shapes and decorated with charming scenes. War was now represented only by a soldier saying goodbye to his family, battles against barbarians or monsters became scarcer; the old popular theme of banquets fell out of favour, and athletes practising wrestling or discus-throwing gave place to young ladies of fashion adorning themselves at their mirrors in the gyneceum, with Loves fluttering around them. The rape of mortal women by gods or heroes became an increasingly popular subject, and one of the characters most frequently represented was Paris, either passing judgment on the beauty of the three goddesses or else, in Helen's boudoir, displaying his grace and the splendour of his Oriental garb. We recognize the refined, somewhat precious atmosphere of a society increasingly aware of spiritual values: we see girls ecstatically dancing, while the mythical poets, Orpheus or Thamyris, take the place of honour once reserved for warriors. It is not surprising that at the same period Euripides was denigrating athleticism and extolling the virtues of the mind.

Whether in imitation of large-scale painting, or merely because fashions derived from the East had introduced among the Athenians a taste for finery which, earlier, more austere generations had condemned, the figures on these vases, particularly the women, are now dressed in richly embroidered draperies heightened with touches of white or bright gold: red-figure painting, formerly so unadorned, thus takes on a gay and lively aspect hitherto unknown. There is here an obvious attempt to emulate large-scale painting and, at the same time, a certain sense of discouragement and humility in the face of such hopeless competition; vase-painters, feeling themselves outstripped, give up signing their works; one of the few potters whose name still survives is Meidias, whose works, in fact, are by no means devoid of value; one of the best known is in London and shows on one side the Rape of the Leukippidai by the Dioscuri and on the other, Herakles surrounded by a charming group of girls, the Hesperides. No less exquisite are the scenes painted by an anonymous artist, known as the Eretria painter, on one of those tiles that spinning women used to place across their knees and thighs to stretch their thread: scenes in the gyneceum, so full of life that one can almost hear the babble of these young women as they adorn themselves.

The social transformation then taking place in Attica, reflected in the sphere of ceramic art by the desire to please an increasingly feminine public, must also have been manifest in larger painting. During the last thirty years of the fifth century two great artists came to the fore, Zeuxis and Parrhasios; neither was an Athenian, and by their way of life as well as by the subjects they chose, they belonged to that rather rowdy younger generation of which Alcibiades is, for us, the typical representative. We can imagine, from the numerous vase paintings of the subject, what Zeuxis' picture of Helen at her toilet must have been like—a very beautiful young woman, half clad, surrounded by maidens as elegant as herself, with her hair elaborately dressed in a knot on top of her head and her garment made of a transparent material, richly embroidered. When a hero was depicted, which was now infrequently the case, he looked—as we are told of Parrhasios' Theseus—'as if he had fed on roses'. An ever more marked concern with the expression of feeling, a more keenly analytic spirit led artists to portray allegorical figures whose significance might be quickly grasped: Demos, for instance, personifying the People, whose face revealed his inconstancy.

Without going so far, vase-painters were adept at representing their characters' feelings. On the white-ground funerary *lekythoi* which were then being produced in large numbers, the dead man often seems to wear a tragic look and his lips are contorted with grief; when we remember the impassivity that is characteristic of funerary *stelai* of the same period, and the restrained grief displayed by the mourners on these, we are tempted to conclude that painters were the pioneers in the study of characterization. In other respects, too, these painters experimented along new lines which were to prove highly fruitful. It was towards the end of the fifth century that the difficult problem of perspective and the third dimension was tackled for the first time. Polygnotos had merely set out his figures vertically; this arrangement in tiers gave only a very faint impression of depth and receding planes. The critics of antiquity mentioned Agatharchos and Apollodorus as innovators in this respect; both of these had been stage designers. Forced by professional requirements to create an illusion of reality and consequently of space, they must have been the first to explore ways of suggesting a receding landscape or architecture behind the figures on the stage. As to their method, the nickname *skiagra-phos* or shadow-maker bestowed on Apollodoros indicates that they gave solidity to their figures by introducing shadows; from this period onward, on engraved mirrors, draughtsmen occasionally emphasized their outlines with fine hatchwork lines corresponding to cast shadows. At the same time, while avoiding the artificial and exaggerated character of Polygnotos' arrangement of figures, painters began to set certain figures slightly back, to make them appear to be in the middle ground; they did not yet realise that distance ought to make these figures smaller, but they had succeeded in adding a three-dimensional effect to their scene.

It is difficult to trace the progress of these discoveries, which presumably was rapid, for by the end of the fifth century, with the collapse of the Athenian empire in 404, an abrupt break occurs in the production of ceramics. For a score of years at least the pottery workshops seem to have closed down: this was probably due less to any real artistic decadence than to the collapse of a market whose prosperity depended largely on Athenian influence abroad and the fortunes of the Athenian navy. The potters' clientèle had not entirely vanished, and certain very precious vases were still exported beyond the Adriatic for a few insistent customers: the Pronomos vase, which shows a flute-player winning a contest, watched by Dionysos and his mistress Ariadne and surrounded by a whole troop of actors, the *amphora* representing the Giganto-machia, probably inspired by a sculptured group or even by the painting inside Athena's shield on the Parthenon, and a few other works, all very carefully executed, allow us to assume that even in the midst of their country's disasters not all the workshops of Athens had closed down.

But the tradition to which they clung was doomed by the progress of large-scale painting. In the fourth century, the Athenian potters only worked for a clientèle that was scattered in the far confines of the Grecian world, for Hellenized barbarians whose orders seemed insignificant by comparison with the demands made in previous centuries by the Etruscans and other inhabitants of Italy. As these barbarians were men of taste, the vases they were sent were in no wise inferior in quality, but it is evident that the decorators were haunted by an ideal which they lacked the technical means to realise. These vase-painters, whose names we do not know, since they never signed their works, had before their eyes pictures executed with all the resources of a vigorously developing art. It is possible that large-scale painters had already learnt how to produce gradations of colour; in any case their palette was far richer than that of the ceramic painters; the latter had presumably supplemented the white and gold already in use at the end of the fifth century with blue and pink, but these were fragile colours that would not stand up to high temperatures or to moisture. Moreover, it was difficult to convey depth and space on vases of the reduced size now imposed by fashion and economic necessity. These fourth century Attic vases, known as Kerch vases since many of them were discovered in the Crimea, are interesting in many respects, particularly because they betray the taste of the time for erotic subjects, because many of their favourite themes imply a concern with mysticism, and because they often anticipate motifs which later sculptors were to adopt and popularize: the squatting Aphrodite, of which our museums provide so many examples and whose origin in statuary does not go back beyond the beginning of the third century, is already pictured on Kerch vases dating from before the middle of the fourth.

This scanty Athenian output is somewhat dwarfed by the enormous mass of vases fashioned and decorated in Southern Italy. In 442 an Athenian colony, Thourii, had been established close to the heel of Italy and pottery workshops had promptly been set up. The colonists, indeed, included a number of potters who went on practising their trade in their new homeland. And almost to the end of the fifth century these Italiote vases, as they are called, were hardly distinguishable from those made in the mother country. But succeeding generations lost contact with Athens, and although they remained faithful to Athenian traditions, the potters' work displays a feeling which is no longer purely Greek. One of their most striking features is that in order to please their somewhat barbarian local clientèle they fashioned a large number of huge vases in a monumental style, overloaded with ornaments. On the bodies of tall *amphorae* and huge *kraters* they display scenes laid out in several registers, one above the other; the figures are not grouped in tiers as in the work of Polygnotos, but form distinct bands even when no framework separates them. Their subjects are often taken from Greek drama, for which the Italians had such a passion that they were said to have set free those Greek prisoners who could delight them by reciting passages from Euripides.

Other vases represent religious themes, related to the cult of Dionysos or of the dead. These are in general somewhat inferior artistically and clumsy in workmanship. The various Italiote schools—Lucanian, Campanian, Apulian—produced few masterpieces. And despite the occasional use of striking colour, their vases tell us little about large-scale painting. They were not meant for export and the customers who bought them had different requirements from those of the Greeks of the preceding centuries.

It must be admitted that neither these Italiote vases nor those of the Kerch group give us any enlightenment about the monumental compositions of contemporary painters. The fourth century was by all accounts the age of painters; the most famous name is that of Apelles, the only artist whom Alexander allowed to paint his portrait, but the critics of the time also praised his rival Protogenes. Their works are known to us only by their titles. However, failing any acquaintance with individual painters, it is possible to gain a glimpse of the art of that time from its reflection in Roman painting, particularly in the works discovered at Herculaneum and Pompeii. The difficulty lies, as we have pointed out, in distinguishing the fourth century element in these eclectic compositions from the painter's own invention, and from what he has borrowed from other styles.

We can also gain some information from certain humble but original works, contemporary with those of the great painters. It was becoming fashionable in the fourth century to pave certain formal reception rooms in private houses with mosaics, usually composed of purely decorative motifs but occasionally showing figured scenes: at Olynthus, a small northern town which Philip of Macedon destroyed in 348, a mosaic has been found showing the Nereids bringing to Achilles the weapons forged for him by Hephaistos, and there is a somewhat later one at Pella in Macedonia representing a lion-hunt. The colours are restricted, but the artists had already learnt to produce an effect of colour gradation. No less interesting, although mediocre in quality, are some paintings which have been preserved on grave *stelai* at Pagasai, near the gulf of Volo. These represent scenes of farewell, like those carved in relief on similar *stelai*, but these scenes are usually situated in an architectural setting, inside a house of which we can see the walls and doors and sometimes even, in the background, a series of rooms. Thus the painter was led to seek effects of distance, almost of perspective, which he had not invented himself, but the models, or at any rate the idea, of which had been provided by the eminent painters whom we know only by reputation. In these scenes—and the same feature is to be found in the Kerch vases—certain figures are shown in attitudes that demand bold foreshortening.

We must also mention as evidence the paintings discovered a few years ago in Bulgaria, on the site of Kazanlak; they adorned one of those vaulted tombs, the tradition of which had persisted in the provinces of Anatolia and the Danubian regions from the Mycenean period to Roman times; the entrance passage and the funerary chamber were entirely covered with frescoes, which happen to have been well preserved. The figured scenes are not highly original: chariot races, banquets in honour of the deceased and his wife; there is nothing remarkable about these. Nor is the execution of these works in any way outstanding. But the very fact that these frescoes were made by simple provincial workmen increases the likelihood of their providing a faithful reflection of the paintings familiar to third century Greeks, and the conception of painting that reigned at the time.

All these minor works, however, are valuable chiefly as landmarks in the evolution of an art whose peak of technical perfection was reached in the paintings of which we have the Roman copies. By studying these we can watch the progress gradually achieved in the rendering of effects of colour, perspective, and gradations of tone. Thus, by comparison with them, we may consider a great mosaic at Naples as being the fairly faithful reproduction of a painting probably executed during the last years of the fourth century. This famous mosaic, *Battle of the Issus*, was discovered in relatively good condition at Herculaneum. The artist has represented the culminating point of the battle: Alexander the Great is face to face with Darius, King of the Persians, threatening him with his lance, Darius is on a chariot drawn by four horses and is gazing with horror at one of his own officers who has rushed forward to protect him and fallen, victim of his loyalty. Alexander is on horseback, full of the excitement of battle. This scene occupies the middle of the composition and forms the centre of a vast tournament between contending armies, whose compact mass seethes in a semi-circle around the edges and in the background; of the most distant horsemen nothing is seen but their spears pointing skyward. A few withered tree-trunks provide the natural setting, according to the old convention already used in archaic times. But the novelty here consists in the impression of space which the artist has succeeded in conveying: certain figures seen from the back seem to be rushing off into the distance, others are shown turning round, with an effect of solidity due to skilful foreshortening, and finally the principal characters are set apart from their armies by a space that gives them prominence, like leading actors in the forefront of the stage. By studying the vases of the fourth century, the engraved mirrors and the minor works we have mentioned, one could easily find the equivalents or at least the immediate precursors of all these innovations. And this entitles us to think that the original reproduced in this Neapolitan mosaic was not far removed in time from these documents, and must have been faithfully copied. Added to which, the mosaicist has deliberately restricted his colours to the four which constituted Polygnotos' palette; now why should he thus have reduced his potentialities of expression in a work which is by no means archaistic, unless out of deliberate faithfulness to the painting he wished to reproduce? We may also note that the portrait of Alexander is singularly lifelike and that, although of course it was not done from life, it seems to date from a period when the features of the great conqueror were still undimmed in people's memories. We can thus consider this mosaic, on the whole, as providing evidence about pictorial art on the eve of the Hellenistic period.

If the picture we have just described did undoubtedly represent the Battle of the Issus—the incident of Darius being saved by one of his officers is mentioned in texts as having occurred during this battle—the author of the composition is certainly unknown. Several names have been suggested, notably that of Philoxenos of Eretria, but none of these was as famous in antiquity as Apelles, Protogenes or Aetion; if fame is any indication of artistic quality, the aesthetic merits of the Neapolitan mosaic, which are even greater than its documentary value, enhance one's regret that so little is known about those who were then considered the greatest masters.

It is useless to enumerate names of painters or paintings which mean nothing to us. It is more profitable to enquire what Roman paintings bear any relation, in subject or treatment, to the development of art subsequent to the death of Alexander. There are many such works; often they borrow from their Greek models only a motif, an isolated figure, a nuance in the expression of feeling. One can trace analogies between the painted figure of a hero, erect and naked, and a sculptured figure by Skopas or one of his school. And here and there a draughtsman has given almost sculptural relief to his figure by the use of lights and shadows. Certain of these Roman paintings are so closely akin to sculptured plaques of definitely Hellenistic style that we are tempted to assume them to be derived from the same model; and such models may well have been paintings, more suitable than reliefs for this particular sort of subject. Almost always they are landscapes, town or country scenes, and these landscapes, far from reproducing reality, spring from the artist's imagination. They remind one of those fanciful 'reconstructions' of nature concocted by painters of our own eighteenth century in their studios.

The nature thus reconstructed is lush and wild, with steep rocks, grottoes, rivers, trees with romantic foliage overhanging complicated specimens of architecture, ruins akin to those in which Hubert Robert was later to delight. These landscapes sometimes provide a setting for human figures, and sometimes the human beings seem merely inessential adjuncts to the natural scene. Of particular interest are the so-called Nilotic landscapes, whose obviously Egyptian origin is shown by the presence of exotic animals, such as hippopotami or crocodiles.

It is most unlikely that the landscapes which served as models to the Roman painters were earlier than the Hellenistic period. On the other hand it is hard to determine the date of a number of other works, some of which offer purely classical features while others are steeped in an atmosphere hardly conceivable before the third century.

This is not the place to discuss the problems raised by the frescoes that adorn the famous Villa dei Misteri at Pompeii. These are generally agreed to illustrate Dionysiac ritual and to be based on a Hellenistic model; but among the numerous figures in this composition, there are some that may date back to the period of Alexander, if not earlier, while others are reminiscent of second century sculptures. It is impossible to state with any degree of certainty when and how these various figures were combined, and whether these rites, so long restricted to initiates, were thus revealed even before the time of the Romans. The skill with which relief is suggested proves, in any case, that the Classicising tendencies manifest here had already begun to appear in sculpture at the dawn of the Hellenistic period.

What strikes us when we consider paintings like those in the Villa dei Misteri is the extreme technical skill, amounting to virtuosity, of the artists of this time. The vividness of expression and attitude in the figures, the felicitous harmony of the colouring, combine to give a reassuring sense of mastery; true, there is a certain absence of spontaneity, and one is tempted to use the term 'academic', yet neither sincerity nor talent are lacking here. The Venus of Milo is academic too, and archaic art has no monopoly of artistic excellence.

It is likely that every *genre* practised in the Hellenistic period was represented in painting as well as in sculpture. The paucity of painted portraits known to us is due, probably, to accident at the moment of discovery, or to the ravages of time; whereas so many cities commemorated their great men with full-length statues or with busts, we have practically no paintings that can be unhesitatingly considered as likenesses of statesmen, poets or even private citizens. The only exceptions are a few hypothetical portraits of philosophers in certain pictures. Curiously enough it is only at a relatively late period, at the beginning of our own era, and in a province remote from the Greco-Roman world, in the oasis of Fayum in Egypt, that portraiture is most adequately represented. But the artistic merit of these portraits is on the whole less than their documentary interest; they are merely likenesses of humble individuals painted on their sarcophagi in accordance with religious ritual. It is extremely probable that, quite apart from these Egyptian customs, in other more central regions, people of importance commissioned great artists to paint their portraits; Alexander had assigned to Apelles the sole privilege of reproducing his features, and his successors, as well as less eminent people, must also have sat for their portraits, along with their families, to their favourite painters.

Conclusion

It would no doubt hardly be necessary to add a summary of the history of painting in ancient Greece, from Minoan to Roman times, if the evolution of that art had followed a regular course. A mere chronological account would make any such conclusion al most sup. nsoerflu

But we have seen that on the contrary the phases of Greek painting, at least according to the evidence we possess, did not follow one another in any logical and coherent fashion. The only two epochs in which one has the impression that the Greeks were painters, rather than primarily draughtsmen, are right at the beginning and right at the end of the history of Hellenic art. The break between the Mycenean world and that which took its place towards the beginning of the first millennium is more noticeable in the history of painting than in any other sphere.

Until then, painting had been the most obvious and natural means of expression for a race of people in whom feeling and sensitivity were dominant; painting alone was a medium flexible enough to render their transient impressions and the bright colours of their world.

After the break made by the Doric invasions, drawing was valued solely for its precision, which made possible the exact definition of ideas and images. It was no longer a springboard for flights of fancy, but on the contrary presented the spectator with a clear-cut, unalterable image. Intellectualism controlled sensation. Can it be claimed that the Hellenistic period revived the tendencies of Minoan times? True, the strictly Classical spirit was modified from the fourth century onward, and reason no longer governed artistic expression as jealously as it had done almost since Archaic times, but it had set an indelible imprint on the Greek spirit; even feelings were cast in a rationalist mould and their expression inevitably took a literary form. Greek painting was never to recover the admirable spontaneity of certain Cretan frescoes, such as that showing the cat stalking a pheasant.

If Greek painting did not follow a logically continuous line in its development, we must point out, nonetheless, that by the end of the second millennium the Cretan ideal had already undergone considerable alteration since Minoan times, through contact with the peoples of the mainland, whose cultural influence spread with the growth of their political power; and the hardening already noticeable in mural or vase-painting in the thirteenth and twelfth centuries led almost imperceptibly to the Geometric style which was to dominate exclusively until nearly the end of the eighth century.

These Geometric and intellectual trends are not mere accidents; they correspond to the deepest element in the Greek mentality; if they had been due merely to an invasion, they would not have resisted the Orientalising wave of the seventh century. But on the contrary the Oriental influence was to vanish as swiftly as it had appeared, and if the Geometric trend was no longer as strictly dominant as in the times immediately preceding the Doric invasion, yet the paramount importance of design, of line, of exact contour as opposed to colour, nuance, shadow and gradation of tone is a sign that a mathematical strictness is indeed part and parcel of the Greek mentality. As has been pointed out, the writers of antiquity seem to speak with more fervour of painting than of any other art; but in fact what appealed to them was the art of drawing, which, even more than that of sculpture, has the power of defining form.

Greek painting

Illustrations

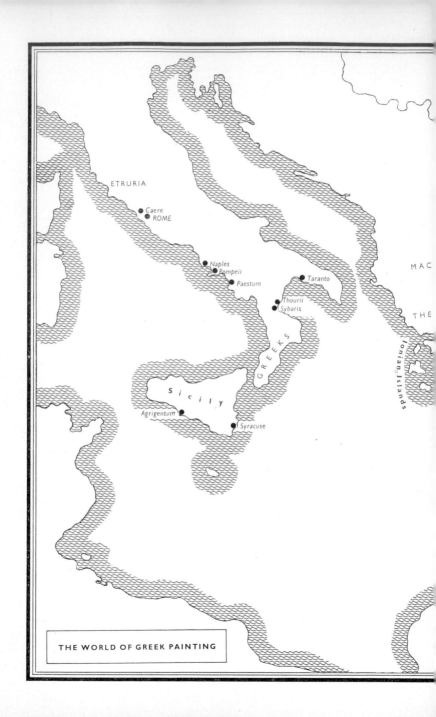

ETRURIA

● Caere
● ROME

● Naples
● Pompeii
● Paestum

● Taranto

● Thourii
● Sybaris

G R E E K S

S i c i l y

Agrigentum ● ● Syracuse

MAC

THE

Ionian Islands

THE WORLD OF GREEK PAINTING

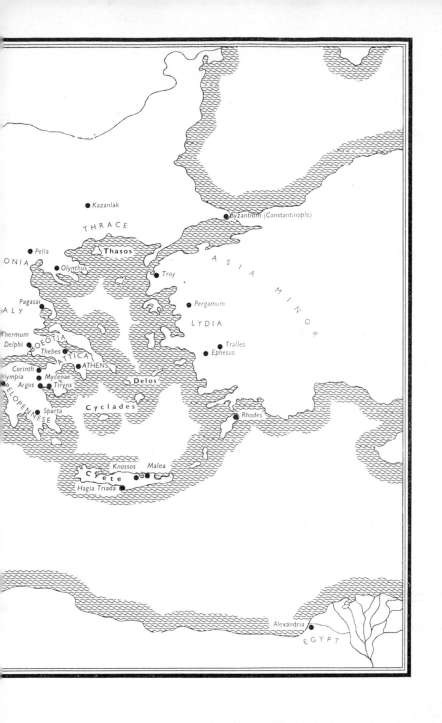

Kazanlak

THRACE

Byzantium (Constantinople)

Pella

Thasos

ASIA

ONIA

Olynthus

Troy

MINOR

Pagasai

Pergamum

ALY

LYDIA

Thermum

Delphi

BOEOTIA

Tralles

Thebes

ATTICA

Ephesus

Corinth

ATHENS

lympia

Mycenae

Delos

Argos

Tiryns

PELOPENNESE

Sparta

Cyclades

Rhodes

Knossos

Malea

Crete

Hagia Triada

Alexandria

EGYPT

1

2

3

4

9

11

13

14

17

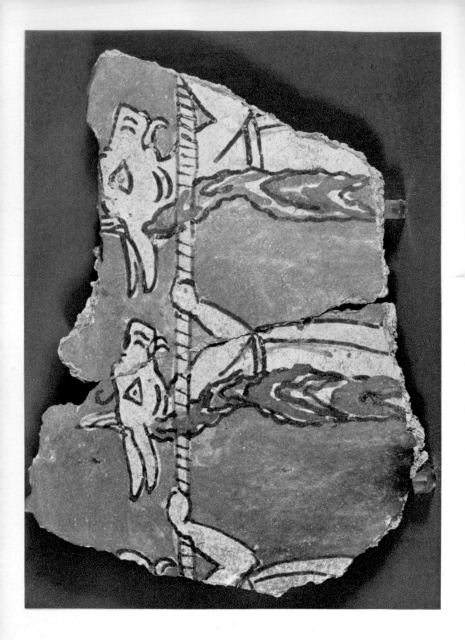

18

24

29

31

33

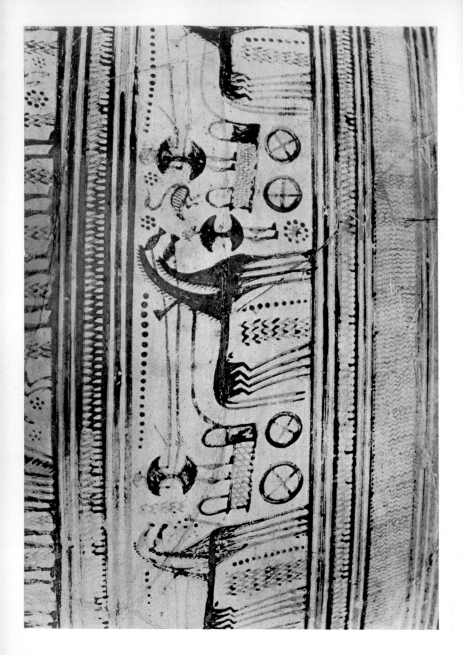

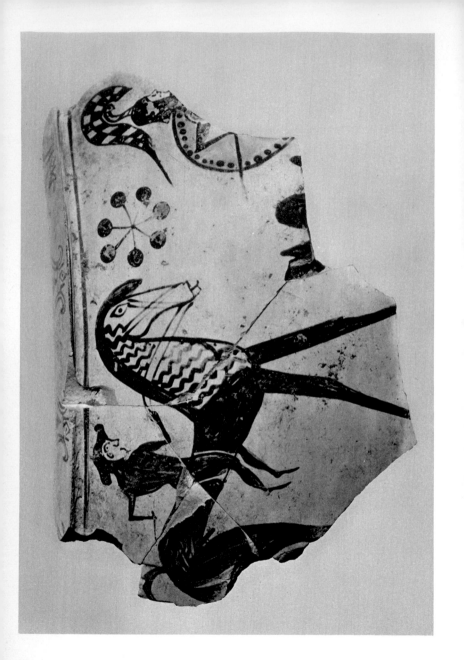

43

46

47

49

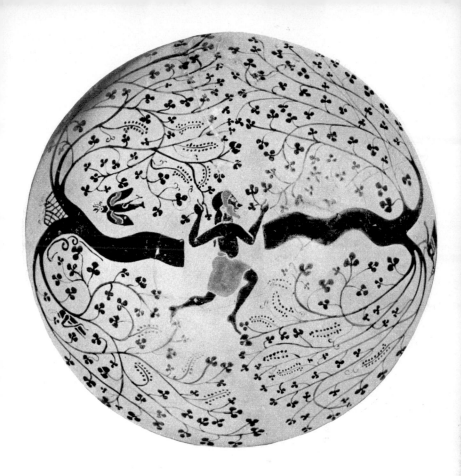

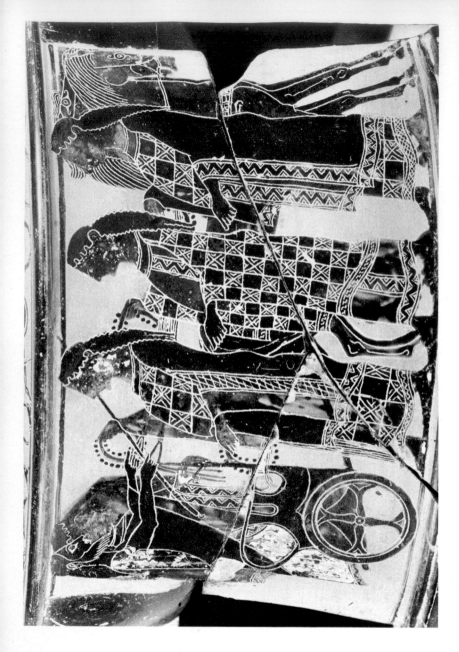

87

93

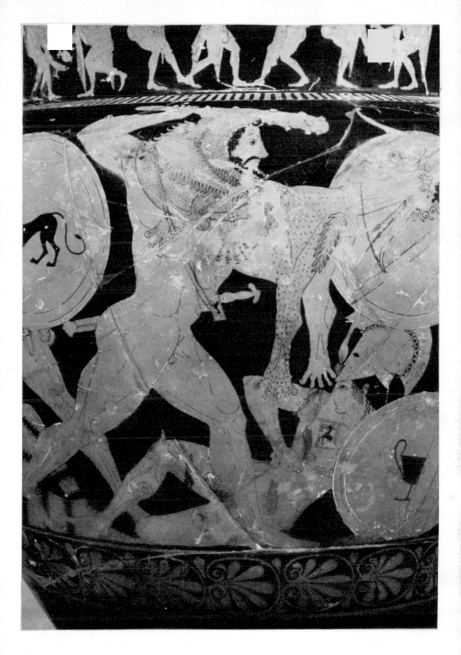

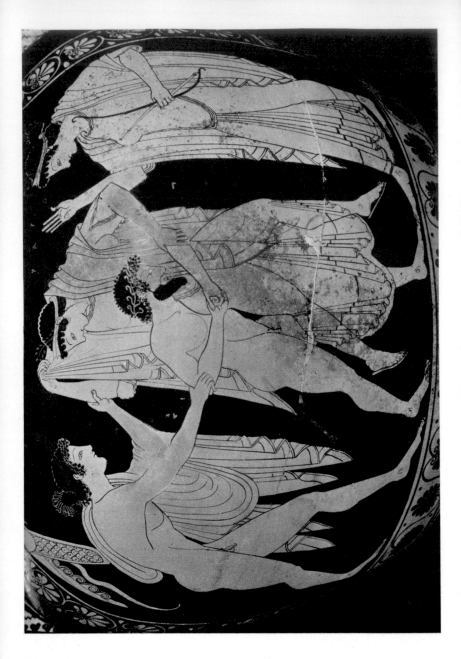

101

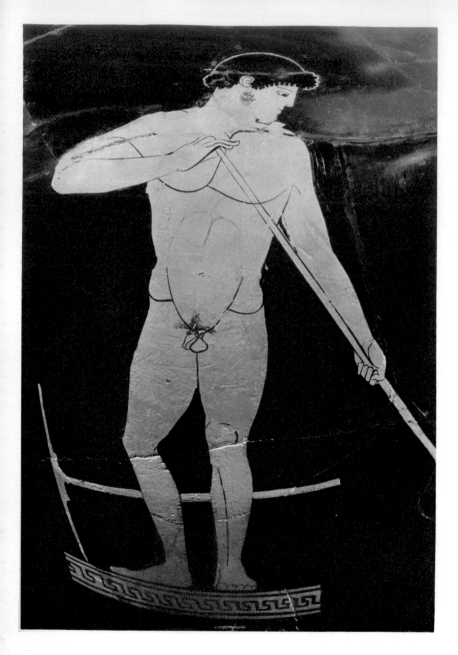

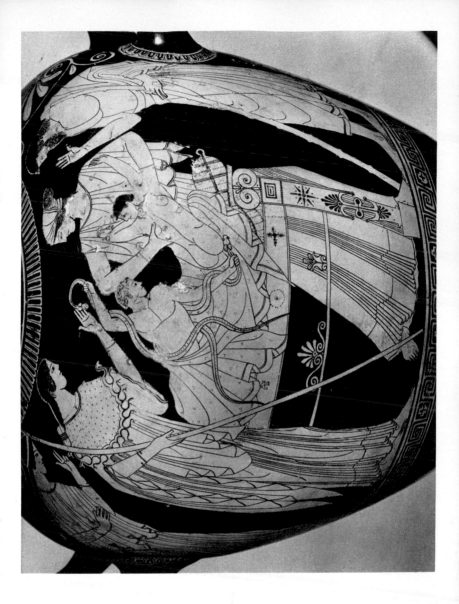

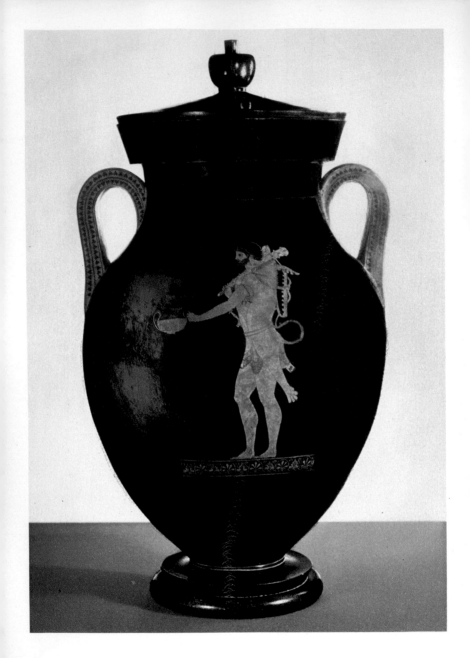

115

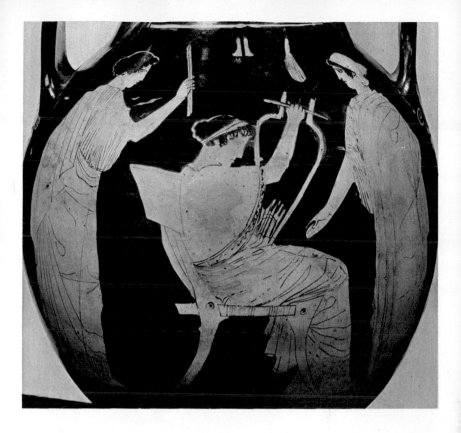

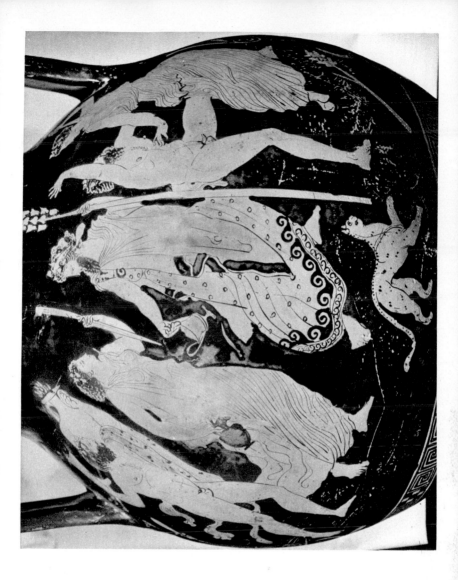

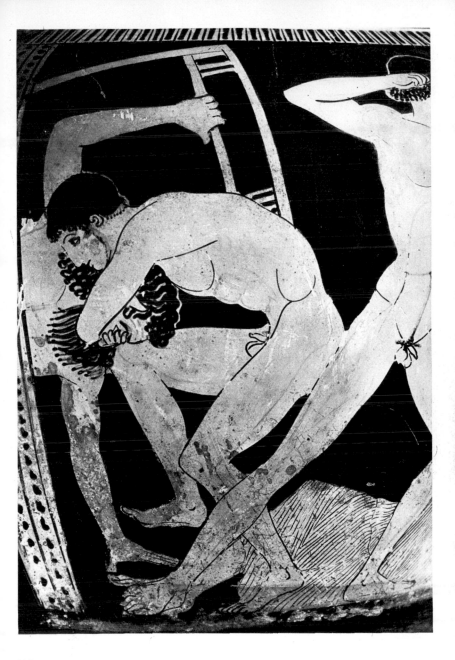

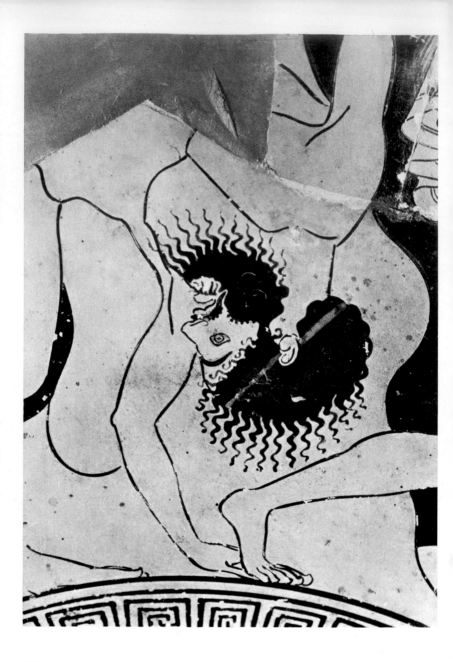

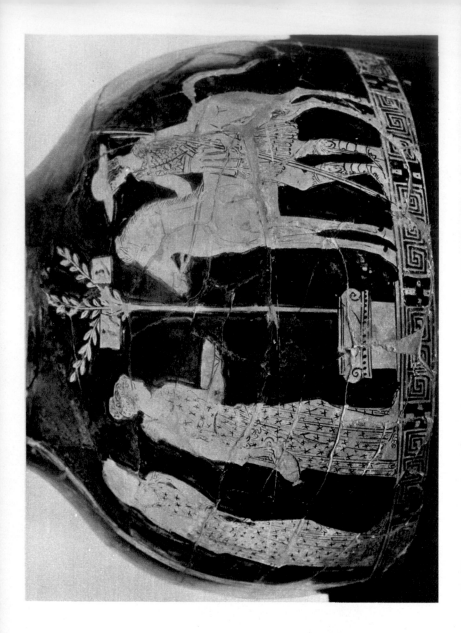

143

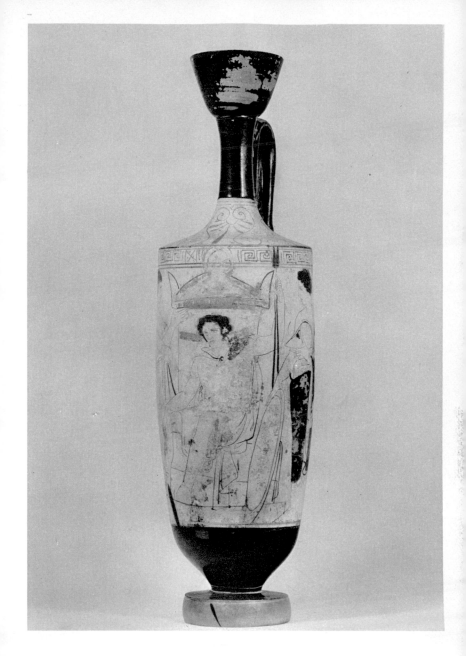

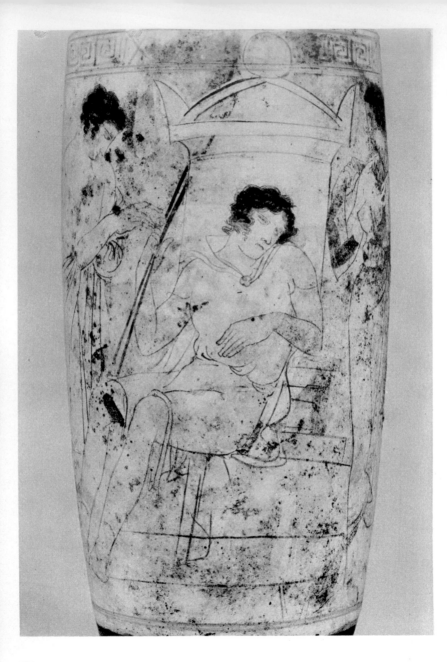

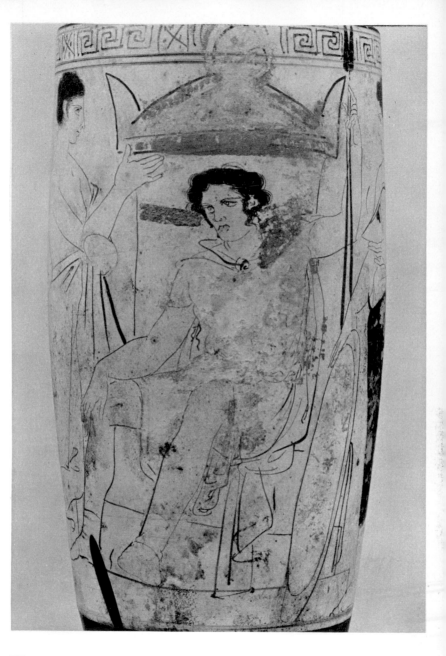

152

153

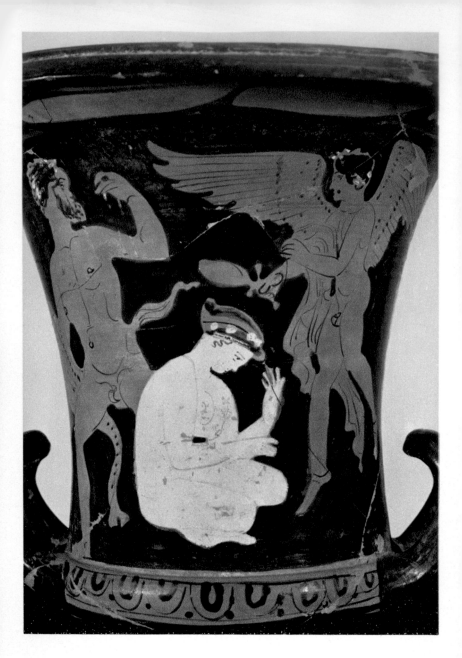

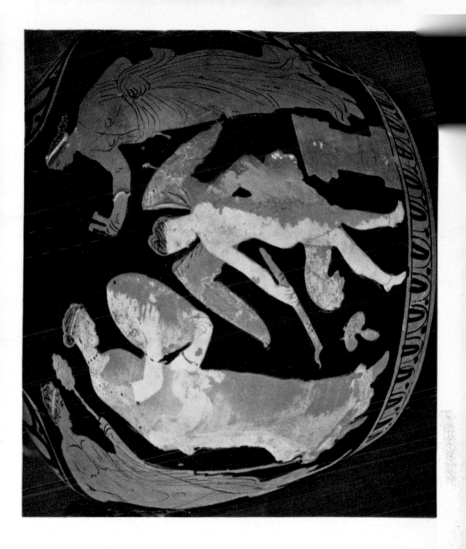

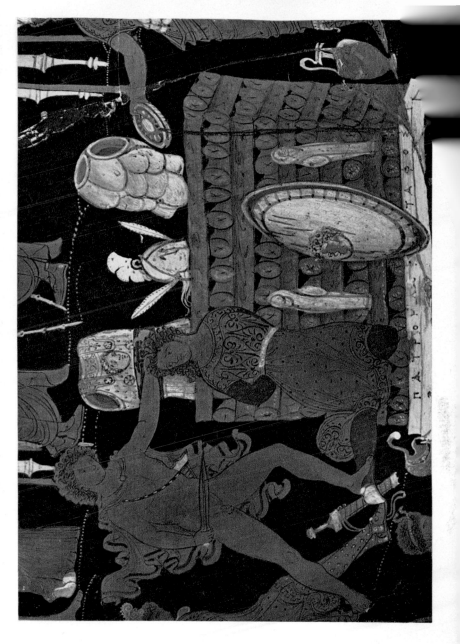

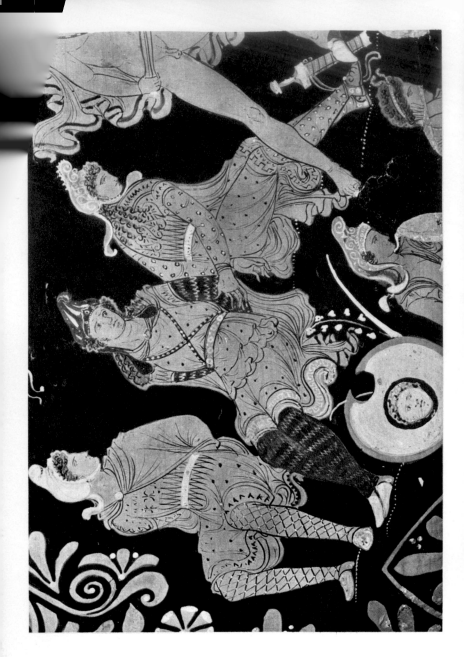

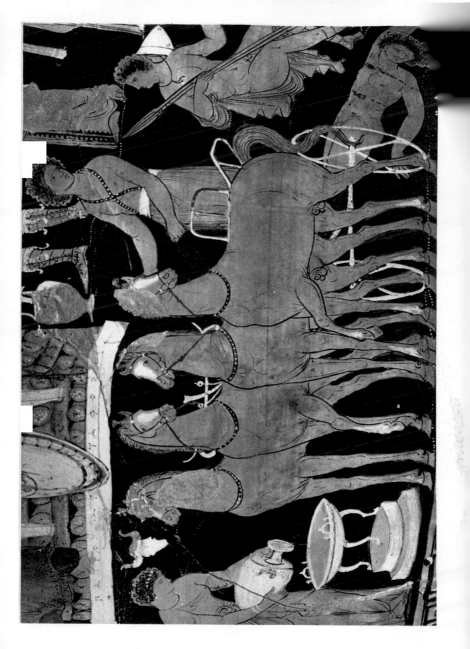

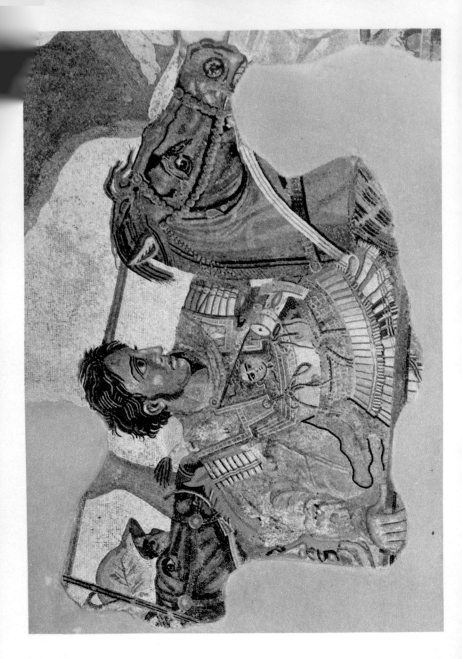

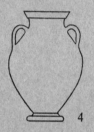
1

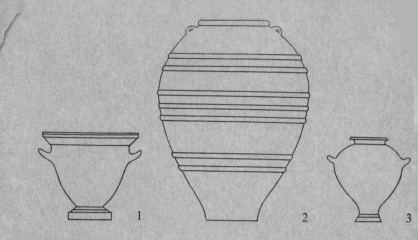
2

3

4

5

6

7

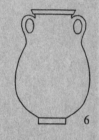
8

9

10

11

12

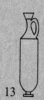
13

The following brief glossary explains the different types of Greek vases:

Vases for containing liquid or grain

1 *krater*: in which liquids were mixed, explaining its wide mouth. The shape and position of its handles vary.

2 *pithos* usually the size of a jar, not decorated. Also a smaller vase with a cylindrical body and very wide mouth.

3 *stamnos*: similar but proportionately smaller.

Vases for transporting liquids

4 *amphora*: generally oval-shaped, with a constricted mouth and small lid.

5 *hydria*: fitted with three handles, serving as a jug to carry water from a fountain.

6 *pelike*: a type of amphora.

7 *oinochoe*: a jug for pouring.

Vases for drinking

8 *cup*: large receptacle on a base of varying height.

9 *styphos* and *cotyle*: equivalents of our bowls

10 *cantharus*: goblet with high-curved handles, usually on a base.

Vases for perfume

11/12 *aryballos* and *alabastron* are narrow flasks, the former oval shaped or swollen in the centre, the latter long and thin. Their bases are sometimes rounded.

13 *lekythos*: used for funerals by the fifth-century Athenians, is long and cylindrical. It has an exaggerated spout.

List of plates